LIZARDS

LIZARDS
BY KAREN GRAVELLE

FRANKLIN WATTS

New York · London · Toronto · Sydney
A First Book · 1991

Cover photograph courtesy of Animals Animals/Stephen Dalton/OSF
Photographs courtesy of: Wade C. Sherbrooke: pp. 2, 3, 17, 19, 43 bottom, 45 top, 47; Irene Heiney: p. 12; C.J. Cole; pp. 14, 35; Devin Scott: pp. 20, 26 top, 32; Karen Gravelle: pp. 24, 26 bottom, 29, 41 bottom, 43 top; Animals Animals: pp. 28, 53, 54 top (all Zig Leszczynski), 38 (Bruce Davidson), 39 (Joe & Carol McDonald), 45 bottom (Hans & Judy Beste), 51 (Richard K. LaVal), 54 bottom (Raymond Mendez); Dr. Walter Auffenberg: p. 40; Steve Dono: p. 41 top.

Library of Congress Cataloging-in-Publication Data

Gravelle, Karen.
    Lizards / by Karen Gravelle.
      p.   cm.—(A First book)
    Includes bibliographical references and index.
    Summary: Discusses lizards and their different survival techniques, such as changing color.
    ISBN 0-531-20026-4
     1. Lizards—Juvenile literature.   [1. Lizards.]   I. Title.
II. Series.
QL666.L2G73   1991
597.95—dc20   91-4665 CIP AC

TO AILEEN CLARK GRAVELLE

CONTENTS

INTRODUCTION

What would your life be like if you were a lizard? If you could press a magic button and become a lizard, you'd find that, in many ways, your concerns would be similar to those of human beings. Lizards, like people, must have a place to live, food to eat, and protection from *predators*. Both lizards and humans must reproduce if future generations are to exist. It's in how they do these things, though, that lizards and people differ. And in some cases these differences are pretty big.

This book will help you to understand what these differences are and why they exist. So, for a little while, let's step inside a lizard's skin and see what life is like.

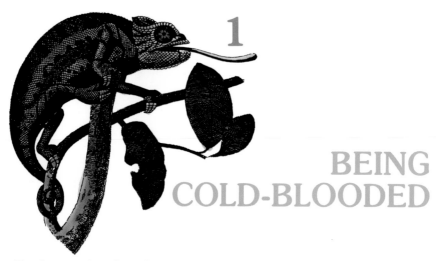

1

BEING COLD-BLOODED

Perhaps the hardest change to adjust to, if you were magically to become a lizard, would be living your life as a *cold-blooded* animal. Reptiles (including lizards), amphibians, fish, and insects are all cold-blooded animals, or *ectotherms*. *Mammals* and birds, on the other hand, are *warm-blooded* animals, or *endotherms*.

The terms cold-blooded and warm-blooded, however, are somewhat misleading. An ectotherm's blood is not always cold. On the contrary, sometimes it can become dangerously hot, far warmer than the blood of endotherms.

Every animal, cold- or warm-blooded, has a particular temperature at which its body works best. Mammals and birds are considered to be warm-blooded not because their bodies are necessarily warmer than those of reptiles, but because they use their own internal sources of heat to maintain the correct body temperature. Warm-blooded animals have an internal thermostat that keeps their bodies constantly heated to that temperature. It doesn't matter whether the environment around them is hot or cold.

In contrast, cold-blooded animals are dependent on heat absorbed from the environment to keep their bodies at the correct temperature. Thus, when a lizard needs to adjust its body temperature, it must move to a cooler or a warmer spot.

If you were a cold-blooded lizard, therefore, you'd have to spend a lot of time and effort regulating your body temperature. As soon as you got up in the morning, you'd have to find a place warm enough to heat yourself up. If you were like most lizards, this would mean basking in the sun.

Because its body does not function well until its temperature rises, a lizard can't move very fast when it first wakens in the morning. In fact, a cold lizard trying to run looks a little like a movie shot in slow motion. While this may seem amusing to us, it's not for the lizard. Until it has warmed up, the lizard can easily be caught by any animal looking for a meal. Thus, lizards usually bask near a rock *crevice* or other safe place so they can escape if threatened.

After it has warmed its body to the correct temperature, however, a lizard must be careful not to let

Having just emerged from the water,
a large monitor lizard warms up on a
rock by Lake Manyara, Tanzania.

its body get too hot. Because cold-blooded animals do not have an internal "safety switch" as warm-blooded animals do, a lizard that stays in the sun will continue to get hotter and hotter. After a mere ten minutes under the blazing desert sun, it will overheat and die.

By constantly moving from sun to shade and back again, lizards keep from getting either too hot or too cold. Being cold-blooded not only influences a lizard's daily movements, it also determines what parts of the world it can inhabit and at what hours it can be active.

Because cold-blooded animals rely on the environment to regulate their body temperatures, most live in places that are warm at least part of the year. Thus, while birds and mammals can live in *arctic zones,* reptiles are generally restricted to *tropical* or *temperate* areas. Not surprisingly, those lizards that live in temperate climates *hibernate* during the winter. Even in the tropics, however, temperatures during the night can be too cold for most lizards. Thus, unlike many species of mammals and birds, few lizards are active after dark.

Although being cold-blooded obviously has some disadvantages, being an ectotherm has certain advantages over being warm-blooded. Because they generate heat internally, warm-blooded animals need a constant supply of fuel to maintain their body temper-

**Because lizards rely on the environment
to heat their bodies, most, like this little
South American teiid, live in warm areas.**

ature. Birds and mammals must eat often and in large
amounts in order to keep their bodies operating. Cold-
blooded animals, on the other hand, use very little, if
any, of their food as fuel to produce heat. Since food
is used up more slowly under these circumstances,
reptiles can go for much longer periods without eating.

2

LOOKING AT THE WORLD

What would you see when you got up in the morning if, like most lizards, you looked at the world through three eyes? Assuming you were a typical lizard, things would look surprisingly the same as they look to you right now. Using two primary eyes, one on each side of the face, lizards see shapes, movements, and colors just as people do.

In fact, good vision is very important to many lizards, particularly those that spend much of their day out in the open. They rely primarily on their eyes to spot prey and predators. Although many mammals do not have good color vision, colors are very important to these lizards. Through differently colored body parts, they signal to other lizards what species they are and whether they are male or female.

A lizard's third eye, however, serves different purposes. Since the third eye is very small—only a tiny spot in the middle of the lizard's forehead—you aren't likely to recognize it unless you know what to look for. Although this eye has a lens and nerves like the lizard's primary eyes, it cannot detect images. Instead, it sees only differences in light and dark. The lizard uses its third eye as a kind of light meter to determine when it has been out in the sun too long and is in danger of overheating.

Some scientists think that the lizard may also be able to see *polarized light* through the third eye. This is a special kind of light invisible to humans but used by birds and bees to navigate over long distances. Perhaps lizards also use their third eye in navigating, but no one knows for sure yet.

While many lizards have good eyesight, two groups have specialized eyes that can do some extraordinary things. One of these groups is the *chameleons*, a family of lizards found mainly in Africa. With huge bulging eyes that resemble Ping-Pong balls glued to their faces, the chameleons are among the strangest-looking lizards in the world.

There is a good reason why a chameleon's eyes protrude as they do. With its eyeballs in this position, the chameleon can swivel them around in a complete half circle. This means it can look behind its back while

A lizard's third, or pineal, eye is
located in the middle of its forehead.
The third eye of a horned toad is
easy to spot because it is surrounded
by white scales.

facing forward! Even more astonishing, the chameleon can move its two eyes independently. It can use one eye to scout in front for food, while pointing the other eye backward to watch for predators.

Geckos, a group of lizards that lives throughout the tropical regions of the world, also have unusual eyes. Unlike most lizards, geckos are active primarily at night. Therefore their eyes have to be able to make the most of the little light that is available then. It's not surprising that a gecko's eyes are much larger than the eyes of most lizards that are active during the day.

But it's the shape of the pupil, not just the size of the eyeball, that makes geckos' eyes so unusual. Instead of the round pupils that humans and other lizards have, geckos have a variety of long, vertical pupils. Some are smooth-sided, like those of a cat. Others, however, are long, scalloped pupils that close to form a line of four tiny pinholes. Each pinhole sends its own image to the *retina* at the back of the eye, where the different images fall on top of one another. In the dimness of dusk or night, a single image may not be bright enough for the retina to pick up. But a combination of four images provides enough light to be visible.

It might be fun to have eyes like a chameleon or a gecko. But you probably wouldn't be too pleased if you woke up tomorrow as a blind *skink* from South Africa. As their name suggests, these lizards can't see

Many geckos have eyes that resemble those of cats. In both cases, the distinctive shape of the pupil helps the animal to see in the dark.

With no external structures, the ears
of lizards look very different from ours.
The ears of this African agamid are the
dark holes at the base of its head.

at all. Since they live underground where eyesight isn't of much use, however, their lack of vision doesn't hamper them.

Lizards have several other ways of surveying the world besides eyesight. Like humans, they have ears and can detect airborne sounds. But while lizards can hear the snarls, growls, chirping, hissing, and singing of other animals, they are remarkably silent themselves. Only the geckos can make vocal sounds. Although some geckos are barely able to produce weak chirps and croaks, others make loud, nerve-racking barks that keep nearby humans awake at night.

Lizards also use their senses of smell and taste to examine the world. In addition to these two senses, lizards, like snakes, have a third chemical sense called the *vomeronasal system.* This sensory system is a little like smell and a little like taste but different from both of them.

You can tell that a lizard is using its vomeronasal system when you see it sticking out its tongue. Although it may appear to be tasting the air or the ground, the lizard is really using its tongue to scoop up chemicals for the vomeronasal organ to detect. Most lizards use the vomeronasal system to some degree, but for those that live in the *leaf litter,* in decaying logs, or under stones where it's difficult to see, the vomeronasal system is especially important in finding food and locating a mate.

3
WHERE TO LIVE? WHAT TO LOOK LIKE?

Where, if you were a lizard, would you live? Considering that you would now be a cold-blooded animal, where, for that matter, *could* you live?

The answer might surprise you. Lizards can live almost anywhere on land. Lizards have made their homes in deserts and jungles, on the banks of rivers and at the edges of the oceans, in caves and at the tops of trees, under leaf litter and in burrows underground, and even in people's homes. While most lizards live in areas that are warm throughout the year, many live in places where winter temperatures are quite cold (although they must hibernate then). One little lizard can even be found as far north as Lapland.

Lizards manage to survive in such varied environments because they are extremely adaptable. Over millions of years, their bodies and their behaviors have evolved to make the best of many different situations. Because of this, a lizard's appearance, as well as the way it acts, depends partly on the place in which it lives.

Burrowing lizards, such as skinks, provide a good example of the ways in which a lizard's body has adapted to its environment. Although skinks exist in large numbers in forests throughout the world, they are not often seen. This is because most of them live hidden under the leaf litter in woods, in decaying logs, or under stones. Many skinks burrow into the earth, and spend much of their time underground.

As a result, skinks' bodies have become smaller and slinkier than the larger, chunkier bodies of many lizards that live above ground. Most skinks are less than 8 inches (20 cm) long, and the biggest, the Solomon Island giant skink, is only 2 feet (.6 m) in length.

Skinks have adapted to their environment in other ways as well. Long legs can get in the way when wiggling underground or slithering beneath rocks. As a result, skinks' legs have become shorter—even disappearing entirely in some species. To protect their eyes from soil particles, many skinks have developed a transparent plate that covers part of the eyeball. Although this cuts down on the skink's eyesight somewhat, vision isn't so important in dim places where it's hard to see anyway. Finally, most skinks have sunken

The long snakelike body and reduced
legs of the alligator lizard are adaptations
that make it easier to travel under
rocks, logs, and leaves.

eardrums. This keeps soil particles from tearing the delicate membrane.

The bodies of lizards that live above ground have adapted to their environment, too. Because they generally have good eyesight and live where they can be seen, many of these lizards have *crests,* helmets, expandable throats, or various colored body parts that they use to identify themselves to other lizards.

Because of the many kinds of surfaces that exist above ground, the legs of lizards that live there have also evolved in different ways. As you've probably experienced when at the beach, walking over loose sand can be difficult. Several kinds of lizards that live in the desert have solved this problem by developing a row of spiny *scales* on each toe. This scaly fringe not only helps the lizard travel quickly and easily over the sand, but makes it easier for the animal to dig in and bury itself when the sun becomes too hot.

Other above-ground lizards spend their lives in trees or on rocky cliffs. Since they have to be good climbers, most of these lizards have strong legs and claws. Some who live in trees have gone a step further in developing special adaptations for climbing. Instead of the usual five toes spreading out from the foot, a chameleon's toes are joined together in bundles, with two toes on the outside and three on the inside of its front feet. On its rear feet, it has three toes on the outside. This ar-

Many lizards that live above ground, where they can be seen, use colors to communicate with each other. The bright, multicolored pattern of this African agamid announces both its species and sex.

The sturdy legs and long claws of the spiny lizard are important in helping it climb trees and rocks.

rangement lets the chameleon grip tree branches as it moves. To help make sure it doesn't fall, the chameleon also has a *prehensile* tail that grips the branch.

The chameleon's feet are designed for tree climbing, but the gecko's special feet permit it to climb smooth surfaces—even glass. These little lizards have no trouble scurrying up a windowpane or dashing across a ceiling. The gecko accomplishes these amazing stunts with the help of ribbed pads on the bottom of its feet. These ribs have microscopic hooks that catch in the tiny bumps that are present on almost all surfaces, including glass. In addition to these special pads, geckos also have sharp claws which are useful in climbing rougher surfaces like trees.

Two tiny lizards of Asia, the Draco and the flying gecko, have developed special body parts that allow them to glide through the air from one tree to the next. These "flying lizards," as they are called, have a wide strip of skin that stretches from their front to back legs. When they jump from a tree, they stretch out their legs and tails, extending the attached *membranes*. Supported by these "wings," they float gently downward.

Very different from the tree-dwelling lizards are the lizards that live near water. Quite a few lizards are good swimmers. The large marine iguana of the Galápagos Islands of Ecuador spends most of its time in the ocean

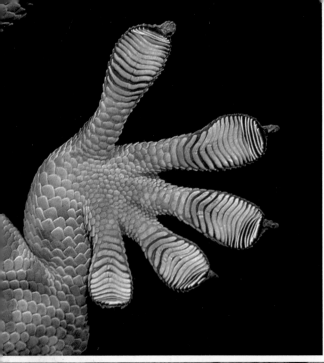

The ribbed pads on the soles of this Tokay gecko's feet help it to cling to smooth surfaces.

The Malaysian draco, or flying dragon, glides through the air supported by flaps of skin extending from its sides.

The Chinese water dragon of Southeast Asia uses its long, powerful tail to swim through jungle rivers.

or on rocks washed by tides, eating algae and sea-weed. Like its relative the common iguana, the marine iguana has a long, powerful tail. These iguanas swim in much the same way as a crocodile or alligator does, with their legs pressed against their bodies and their powerful tails propelling them through the water.

While the marine iguana and the common iguana live in the Western Hemisphere, there are water-loving lizards in the Eastern Hemisphere as well. The big Malayan *monitor* and the Nile monitor are both able to stay under water for long periods. Although no one has yet clocked the Malayan monitor, the Nile monitor can stay submerged for an hour.

In comparison to the lizards that swim in the water, the basilisk lizards of tropical America and the East Indian water lizards are famous for their activities *above* water. Both of these lizards live on riverbanks and have fringed toes. These fringes help the lizards to travel in a most unusual way. When frightened, they stand on their hind legs and run straight across the top of the water!

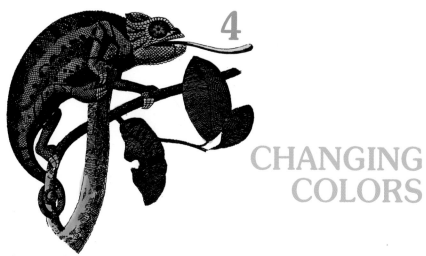

4

CHANGING COLORS

A number of lizards can change their colors in response to certain situations. But no lizard changes colors just on a whim.

The colors of many *iguanid* and *agamid* lizards, for example, change according to the temperature or amount of light the lizard is exposed to. Certain lizards in both families become dark at low temperatures and light at high ones. The darker skin absorbs heat more effectively, helping the animals to raise their temperatures more quickly. As they warm up and need less heat, the color of their bodies becomes lighter.

Early in the morning, after the sun has begun to climb, the spiny lizard emerges from its sleeping place. Its sluggish movements and coal black color indicate how cold it is. Usually, the lizard drags itself onto a warm rock so that it can absorb heat from the stone

Tiny grains of pigment in the skin of
many agamid and iguanid lizards
spread out when the animal is cold,
giving it a black color that absorbs
heat. The patches of blue visible on
this agamid's head and legs indicate
that it's beginning to warm up.

as well as from the sun. Carefully turning its back toward the sun, so that the light falls on as much of its body as possible, the lizard basks, keeping a watchful eye out for danger.

After about twenty minutes, its body starts to become lighter in color and some of its markings can be seen. The lizard begins to move around more on the rock, another sign that it is warming up. Soon its distinctive coloring is clearly visible. Its black collar; black and white back; and bright blue throat, sides, and tail tell what species it is and that it's a male.

What makes the spiny lizard's colors change this way? The change from dark to light is determined by microscopic grains of black *pigment* present in certain cells of the lizard's skin. When these black grains are spread out in the cells, the lizard appears dark. When the animal warms up, the black grains become concentrated in the centers of the cells, allowing the other colors to become visible.

Of all lizards, chameleons are the most famous for their ability to change color. But their reputation for being able to match any color they are placed against is undeserved. Each type of chameleon has only a few colors it can become and, like the iguanids and agamids, these colors are determined by temperature and light, not by background.

The Ituri chameleon provides a good example of

the colors a chameleon can assume. Depending upon the light and temperature around it, this chameleon can go from very pale yellowish green to forest green with large black spots, to olive green marked with black, to very dark brownish green with no spots at all.

The chameleon's color changes happen in a different way than those of the spiny lizard, however. The color cells in a chameleon's skin occur in different layers. These cells can move within each layer, causing various colors and patterns to appear. When yellow color cells of one layer move over blue cells in the layer below, for example, the chameleon's skin looks green.

Even though the changes it can make are limited, the chameleon is usually well camouflaged. Since green and brown are the most common colors in the tropical forest where it lives, the Ituri chameleon always resembles at least some part of the tree on which it's perched.

Temperature and light are not the only things that can cause a lizard's colors to change. A lizard's emotions can sometimes cause its colors to change as well. During combat, many male agamid lizards change color rapidly, depending upon whether they are winning or losing. For example, the Indian bloodsucker (which gets its name from its color, not its eating habits) turns red when victorious and remains brownish or grayish when beaten.

The red color of this male skink's head intensifies during the breeding season.

While it may seem hard to imagine changing your colors depending on whether you've won or lost a fight, you don't have to become a lizard to experience what this is like. People change colors because of their emotions too. When you blush because you're embarrassed or angry, you're doing just what some lizards do.

5

FINDING FOOD

If you were a lizard, chances are good that insects would be your favorite food. While some lizards are strictly plant eaters and others prey on different animals, the majority of lizards are *insectivorous*. Two lizards, the horned toad of the United States and its look-alike, the moloch of Australia, eat primarily one kind of insect, ants. But most lizards are not so particular—spiders, beetles, grasshoppers, anything will do.

Many of the insect-eating lizards are sit-and-wait predators. They don't stalk their prey but wait motionless in one place until a potential meal walks by. Then they dart from their perch and grab the insect with their jaws.

Because these lizards rely solely on their mouths to catch and hold onto prey, their jaws and teeth have to be very strong. The spiny lizard's bite, for example, is strong enough to support the weight of its entire body for at least ten minutes. To match this lizard's accomplishment as a human being, you would have to be able to hang by your teeth from a pole for ten minutes.

Although most predatory lizards capture their food by rushing up to it and grabbing it between their jaws, chameleons have developed a way of "shooting" their meals down. Perched in a tree with its strange toes gripping a branch, the chameleon's bulging eyes swivel forward and backward, looking for its next meal. Once it has spotted an insect, the lizard focuses both eyes forward and begins to creep ever so slowly toward its intended prey. Inch by inch, it approaches the insect, then stops. Suddenly, the chameleon shoots a tremendously long tongue from its mouth. Aimed with deadly accuracy, the sticky tip strikes its insect target. In an instant, the chameleon then retracts its tongue with the insect attached, and swallows its meal.

The larger the lizard, the more food it must eat. Fortunately for the lizard, the larger it is, the bigger the prey it can catch. For example, two *helodermatids,* the Gila monster and the beaded lizard, eat the eggs of birds and reptiles, as well as baby mammals and nestling birds. Since these foods can't run or fly, the lizard doesn't have to rely on speed to capture them. It just walks up and starts eating.

Using its prehensile toes to grip the branch, the chameleon spots insects with its swiveling eyes, then captures them with its long, sticky tongue.

While they may not have to do much to catch their food, Gila monsters and beaded lizards do have to find it in the first place. To do this, they rely on their sense of smell and the vomeronasal organ to track their prey. Even when an egg or nestling is clearly visible a few feet away, these lizards will trace the odor track that leads to the food, even if this takes them well out of their way.

The big tegu, a *teiid* lizard of Colombia and Brazil, is another lizard that includes eggs in its diet. Called the "egg thief" because of its fondness for chickens

and their eggs, it actually relies more on frogs, lizards, and other small creatures for food.

Monitor lizards, which inhabit Africa, southern Asia, the East Indies, Australia, and the Polynesian islands, can sometimes reach 5 or 6 feet (1.5 or 1.8 m) in length. As you might expect, these lizards can prey on much larger animals. The Malayan monitor will eat almost anything it can get its jaws around, including rats, eggs, fish, crabs, frogs, birds (especially chickens), and even decaying meat. The Nile monitor has a fondness for crocodile eggs, and will tear up nests to get at them.

The biggest monitor, and the most fearsome lizard of all, is the Komodo Dragon, which lives on a few

Eggs are a favorite food of the poisonous Gila monster.

isolated islands in the East Indies. At 300 pounds (136 kg) and 10 feet (3 m) in length, a full-grown Komodo Dragon can eat just about any animal it comes across, including pigs, goats, and deer. These giants have even been known to ambush water buffaloes.

Not all large lizards are meat eaters, however. The largest skinks, iguanids, and agamids are all vegetarians. The 3 to 5 foot (.9 to 1.5 m) common iguana, for example, eats a variety of leaves, blossoms, buds, and fruits, while its slightly smaller relative, the land iguana of the Galápagos Islands, prefers cacti. Finally, the only lizard that uses the sea as a habitat, the marine iguana, feeds solely on algae and seaweed, sometimes diving deep to the ocean floor where it remains, feeding, for up to an hour.

The huge Komodo dragon is a skilled predator, even attacking humans on occasion.

Many large lizards
are vegetarians.
The land iguana
can usually be found
near cactus, its
favorite food.

The marine iguana is
the only lizard that gets
its food from the sea.

6

AVOIDING DANGER

Although finding food is an important matter for all lizards, it's just as important for them not to become someone else's dinner. Few small lizards can win a face-to-face fight with a larger animal, but they have other ways of protecting themselves. For the average lizard, camouflage is the best defense. As long as it stays still, a lizard can be very difficult to see. Since the brightly colored parts of its body tend to be on the underside, these colors aren't visible when the animal is flattened against a tree or a rock.

Once spotted by a predator, a lizard's best defense is to flee. Most lizards are very fast and can zip up a tree or into a rock crevice in a flash. Some gain extra speed by standing on their hind legs and running *bipedally* when pursued. The fastest of all, the zebra-tailed lizard, can reach speeds of up to 18 miles (29 km) per hour.

As long as it doesn't move,
this lizard easily blends
into its surroundings.

Like this roadrunner, many mammals,
birds, and reptiles find lizards a
perfectly acceptable meal.

Even when a predator catches up to a lizard, the lizard still has some tricks. The most famous of these is the detachable tail. The tails of most lizards snap off when grabbed, leaving the predator with a mouthful of scales while the lizard itself escapes. The tails of glass snakes (a kind of lizard in spite of its name) are even more easily broken, shattering into several wiggling pieces. By the time the predator quits chasing these decoys, the glass snake is long gone. Luckily, lizards with detachable tails can grow new ones to replace those they've lost.

Other small lizards have developed different ways to discourage predators. Two lizards from Australia, the bearded lizard and the frilled lizard, pretend to be bigger than they are. Both have pointy scales or scaly membranes along their throats and necks. When threatened, they open their mouths and extend their scales. Suddenly the lizard is transformed into an animal twice its previous size, and the predator finds itself looking down an enormous mouth fringed with sharp spines. If the predator isn't much larger than the lizard, it usually reconsiders and looks for food elsewhere.

The chuckwalla from the southwestern United States has another defense mechanism. Like many lizards, it crawls into narrow rock crevices to escape its enemies. Once inside, however, it blows itself up like a balloon, firmly wedging its body between the rocks.

Although losing a tail looks like it would hurt, it doesn't seem to be painful to the lizard. This gecko's stump will soon heal, and a new tail will grow to replace the old one.

The expandable frill along its neck makes the little frilled lizard of Australia look larger and more ferocious than it actually is. This bluff often fools enemies into backing down.

No matter how hard a predator tugs at it, the chuckwalla is immovable.

Two little lizards, the alligator lizard from the western United States and the Deland's lizard from Africa, take advantage of the fact that snakes swallow their prey head first. If a snake seizes the lizard by any part other than its head, the lizard bends over and grabs one of its own hind legs in its mouth. The snake works its jaws around to the lizard's head, so that it can begin to swallow the lizard. But there's no end point where the snake can start, only a closed circle. Even if the snake tries to swallow the lizard tail first, it still can't find a place to begin.

For other small lizards, the motto could be, "If all else fails, do something disgusting." When caught, some alligator lizards, glass snakes, and slow worms (a lizard, regardless of its name) produce a smelly substance from their rear ends which they try to rub on their enemies.

Perhaps the weirdest defense of all, however, is one used by the horned toad of the U.S. desert southwest. When frightened, these little lizards squirt blood from their eyes. How this wards off predators is a mystery, but some scientists think the blood may be irritating to the eyes of small mammals. It isn't of much use against humans, however.

Given a choice, lizards usually try to escape con-

No matter what it looks like,
neither the lizard nor the person is hurt.
In an attempt to drive the human away, the
horned toad squirted blood at him
from its eyes.

frontations with their enemies. Larger lizards, however, are more willing and able to fight if they have to. The common iguana, a lizard that lives in the tropics of the Western Hemisphere, has a powerful 3-foot-long (.9 m) tail which it uses as a whip. One well-aimed whack of this tail can knock a small dog down. Unfortunately, humans are the iguana's most dangerous predator, and its tail is of less use against them.

Because of their size, monitor lizards also have less to fear from other animals. When cornered, a 5-foot (1.5-m) Malayan or Nile monitor with its strong jaws, daggerlike claws, and whiplike tail can be a dangerous opponent. It's no wonder that the only predators willing to tangle with them are humans, crocodiles, birds of prey, and large carnivorous mammals.

There are three lizards, however, that have little to fear from predators. One of these is the huge Komodo Dragon. As the biggest flesh-eating animal on the islands where it lives, the Komodo Dragon is safe from all but armed humans.

The other two lizards, the Gila monster of the southwestern United States and nearby Mexico and the beaded lizard of western Mexico, are not very large. But these two lizards are safe for another reason: They are the only *venomous* lizards in the world. Unlike snakes, which have *fangs* on their upper jaws, these helodermatids have grooved teeth. Thus, venomous

lizards can't strike the way a rattlesnake or cobra can. Instead, they must grip an enemy tightly with both jaws and chew, giving the venom a chance to flow into the bite wound.

For this reason, Gila monsters and beaded lizards have to have very strong jaws. In fact, a major problem in treating helodermatid bites is getting the lizard to let go. Sometimes pliers are needed to pry the lizard's jaws open!

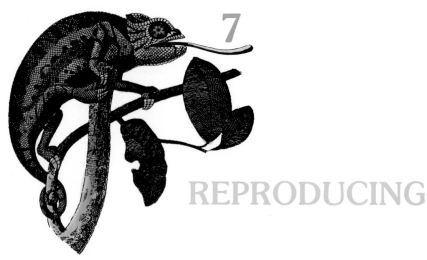

7

REPRODUCING

What is it like for a lizard to find a mate? For male lizards, it is a lot of hard work. Males must compete with each other for females, and the competition can sometimes be fierce!

In many lizard species, these battles have become ritualized. For example, when the little male anole spots a rival, he puffs out his *dewlap,* a large piece of colored skin from his neck, and bobs his head. This is a signal telling the other male to get out of the area. Often, the second male returns the challenge and the two square off, extending their dewlaps, bobbing rapidly, and approaching each other with their mouths open. Usually, this demonstration does the trick, and one of the contestants backs down.

Although these bobbing battles may seem like a strange way to determine the winner, they make a lot

Male anole lizards extend colored
dewlaps from their throats as a warning
to other males to stay away.

of sense. By settling the competition this way, neither lizard actually gets hurt.

Other lizards, however, really do fight. Two male *lacertids* will charge at each other, biting and tearing each other's skin. Skinks also draw blood when they fight, and some males probably die from their injuries.

Defeating rival males is only half the battle, however. In order to mate, the male lizard still has to get a female to cooperate. Many males ask females to mate by using signals that are very similar to the ones used in contests with other males. If the female isn't interested, she merely scurries away. Fortunately, most males eventually attract a willing female.

Once mating is over, the male's work is done. However, depending on her species, the female must now either find a place to lay her eggs or must carry the young in her body until they are ready to be born. Most lizards lay eggs, and some pick unusual places to do so.

The Nile monitor and the tegu both lay their eggs in large, moundlike termite nests. After ripping a hole in the nest with her claws, the lizard deposits her eggs and leaves. The termites swiftly repair their damaged home, sealing the lizard eggs inside where they are safe from predators. Of course, the baby lizards must dig their way out when they hatch.

Common iguanas dig burrows in sandy soil in which to lay their eggs. Since the best nest sites are scarce,

females compete with one another for nesting places in the same way that male iguanas compete for mates.

With very few exceptions, lizards pay no attention to their eggs after they are laid. In one group of skink species, however, the female remains near her eggs, coiling her body around them or lying among them. Since she dashes off at the first sign of danger, the skink isn't exactly guarding the eggs, although her presence may discourage animals that are too small to hurt her but big enough to eat the eggs. She cares for the eggs by turning them periodically so that no single area on the egg gets too damp and rots.

The female five-lined skink is one of the few lizards that tends its eggs. These eggs have already started to hatch.

Appearances can be deceiving. Baby lizards are totally independent from birth, and their parents do not take care of them. This adult chameleon just happened to make a convenient perch for the younger animal.

The female whiptail lizard, seen here gobbling down a grasshopper, is one of several species that can reproduce without the help of males.

A few lizards do not lay eggs but instead give birth to live-born babies. These lizards all live in colder climates where the temperatures are too cool to permit eggs to survive outside the mother. By keeping them inside her body, the lizard can provide her eggs with enough heat to develop.

Finally, the females of a few lizard species can do something no mammal or bird can—have offspring without the help of a male! Among these special females are some whiptail lizards that live in the southwestern United States and Mexico. Since the young of these females have no father, they inherit all their traits from their mother. That means, of course, that they are all female. In fact, these species have no males. Impossible as it may seem, if you were one of these amazing females, each of your babies would not only be your daughter but your genetically identical (although younger) twin as well!

8

WATCHING LIZARDS

Although it might be fun, there is no magic button you can press to become a lizard. Therefore, the next best way to discover what a lizard's life would be like is to spend some time watching one of these animals.

Most lizards do not make good pets. When observed in their natural habitat, however, lizards can be fascinating. Field guide books can tell you not only what kinds of lizards live in your area, but what they look like and where in particular they can be found. Since most lizards will run away if you get too close, bring a pair of binoculars with you so that you can watch them from a distance.

If you live in Florida or the southwest United States, you may even be able to watch lizards in your own home or at least in your backyard. Anoles and spiny lizards, for example, find living near humans very attractive. There's always a supply of insects to eat and certain predators, such as snakes, are likely to avoid these areas.

From what you've read here, you can probably tell what the lizards you watch are doing and why they behave the way they do. So, grab your binoculars and go have a look!

GLOSSARY

Agamids—medium-sized lizards living in the tropical and temperate areas of the Eastern Hemisphere; scaly and often brightly colored with unusual crests, frills, etc.; active in the daytime

Arctic zone—the region around the North Pole

Bipedally—walking or running on two feet

Burrowing—digging a hole in the ground for shelter

Chameleons—small lizards found almost exclusively in Africa; known for their extremely long tongues, which they use to shoot down prey, and their eyes, which swivel independently to look both forward and backward

Cold-blooded—having body temperature dependent on the temperature of the surrounding environment

Crest—a scaly structure on the head, back, or tail

Crevice—a narrow opening

Dewlap—a flap of skin hanging from the necks of some lizards and other animals

Ectotherm—a cold-blooded animal

Endotherm—a warm-blooded animal

Fang—a long, sharp tooth

Geckos—small to medium-sized lizards inhabiting tropical areas throughout the world; primarily nocturnal; the only lizards that make vocal sounds

Helodermatids—sluggish, medium-sized lizards found in the southwestern United States and Mexico; the only poisonous lizards in the world

Hibernate—to pass the winter in a dormant, or sleeping, state

Iguanids—small to large-sized lizards inhabiting tropical and temperate areas of the Western Hemisphere, Madagascar, and the Fiji Islands. Similar in many ways to the agamids of the Eastern Hemisphere, iguanids are active in the daytime and are often brightly colored with crests and dewlaps.

Insectivorous—relying primarily on insects for food

Lacertids—small to medium-sized lizards found throughout Europe, Asia, and Africa; in general appearance, resemble the teiid lizards of the Western Hemisphere

Leaf litter—the blanket of fallen leaves underneath trees and shrubs

Mammals—animals that nurse their young with milk from mammary glands

Membrane—a thin, soft but strong layer (or layers) of skin

Monitors—small to very large aggressive lizards found in the tropics of Africa, Asia, and Australia

Pigment—a substance that gives color to something

Polarized light—light waves that vibrate in a definite pattern and are not visible to human beings

Predator—an animal that preys on and eats other animals

Prehensile—able to grasp objects by wrapping around them

Retina—the part of the eye that receives the image formed by the lens

Scales—small, flat, rigid plates forming the outside coverings of fish, snakes, and lizards

Skinks—small, slinky, secretive lizards that inhabit the leaf litter of forests in both the Eastern and Western hemispheres. Because many skinks spend much of their lives underground, their bodies have adapted to underground living.

Teiids—a family of lizards distributed from Maryland and Wisconsin to Chile; perhaps the lizard family with the greatest variety of habitats

Temperate zone—the area between the tropics and the Arctic in the Northern Hemisphere, and between the tropics and Antarctica in the Southern Hemisphere

Tropical—located in the area around the equator

Venomous—poisonous

Vomeronasal system—a sensory system that detects chemicals in the environment; similar to smell and taste

Warm-blooded—having body temperature internally regulated

FOR FURTHER READING

Behler, J., and F. King. *Audubon Society Field Guide to North American Reptiles and Amphibians.* New York: Knopf, 1979.

Bender, Lionel. *Lizards and Dragons.* New York: Gloucester Press, 1988.

Carr, A. *The Reptiles.* New York: Time-Life Books, 1963.

Harrison, Virginia. *The World of Lizards.* Milwaukee, Wisconsin: Gareth Stevens, 1988.

Schnieper, Claudia. *Chameleons.* Minneapolis, Minnesota: Carolrhoda Books, 1989.

INDEX

ABOUT THE AUTHOR

KAREN GRAVELLE, Ph.D., has a great affection for lizards, having studied their behavior in the American Southwest and the West Indies for her doctorate degree. She now lives in New York City and works as a free-lance writer and photographer specializing in books for children and adolescents. Ms. Gravelle is the author of the Franklin Watts book *Understanding Birth Defects.*